STEAM MEMORIES

SCARBOROUGH

HEYDAY OF THE HOLIDAY TRAINS

ISBN 978-1-907094-56-9

INTRODUCTION

The post-war years leading up to 1963 saw many new trends both economical and social. Public transport, especially the railways, started to pick up the thread of the seaside traffic lost in 1939 and in doing so the newly founded British Railways embarked on a programme of excursion and holiday trains to resorts all over the country. Amongst the more popular destinations in the north of England serviced by BR was Scarborough which was reachable for a day trip by almost 25% of the British public, mainly those living in the industrial heartlands of Yorkshire and east Lancashire. However, there were those who went to Scarborough from further afield such as Glasgow and Birmingham but these visitors stayed for a week or more and were catered for by BR's holiday trains; slightly more up-market in that the trains themselves were made up from corridor stock rather than the 'leg crossing' non-corridor suburban stock usually provided for day-trippers.

The 1950s saw this particular traffic reach a peak and by the end of the decade social trends and personal finance changed insomuch that motor vehicles started to become the preferred mode of transport for British families. The result was a decline in excursion and holiday traffic on BR to the point, nowadays, where it does not exist.

This album is a photographic celebration of the rail traffic serving Scarborough during that magic decade of excursions – the Fifties – as seen through the lens of one photographers' camera, Ron Hodge.

To compliment the train scenes we have included a short history of Scarborough engine shed and its locomotive allocation from 1923 to closure. Enjoy the memories of the images herein because they are now pure history.

(cover) **This is Scarborough. B16/3 No. 61449 is turned on the 60ft turntable in the engine shed yard, 30th April 1955.**

(previous page) **It wasn't just the last decade of steam which saw filth envelope BR's locomotive fleet. A rather grubby looking Doncaster based V2, No.60857, approaches Scarborough in June 1954 with an excursion from Bolton-on-Dearne. Just passing the locomotive depot, the route for the train is set for an arrival at Londesborough Road station. The eleven coaches making up the train are a typical mix of vehicles for the period - anything will do as long as it rolls.**

Printed and bound by The Amadeus Press, Cleckheaton, West Yorkshire
First published in the United Kingdom by Book Law Publications, 382 Carlton Hill, Nottingham, NG4 1JA

Londesborough Road station was just a quarter mile south of Scarborough (Central) and was used mainly for excursion traffic during the summer season. BR Class 5MT No.73065 has just left Central station with the 12.38 p.m. train to York on a somewhat cool Wednesday, 3rd November 1954 and is passing the quiet platforms of the former whilst putting out a nice clean exhaust. The 4-6-0 was, at this time, based at Sheffield Millhouses depot and was a fairly new arrival there (ex Derby works and the first of a batch of ten for the LM Region) although its external condition would have the observer believe it had been at 19B for months rather than approximately three weeks. As part of a Leeds Holbeck diagram, the CL.5 - obviously seconded by Holbeck - had worked into Scarborough with the 8.42 a.m. train from Bradford (Forster Square). The BR1C tender with its 9-ton coal capacity made this engine an ideal candidate for duties such as this and relieved the Standard 5 of having to visit a motive power depot during its travels for the purpose of coaling.

The following day the 12.38 p.m. York train, seen departing platform No.3 in grand style, had Holbeck Stanier Class 5, No.44821, in charge. Later in the month No.44821 was transferred to Saltley so that its chances of visiting Scarborough again would be pretty slim.

Whilst engaged on permanent way duties, A8 No.69886 simmers on a siding adjacent to Falsgrave signal box opposite the junction of the coast line from Whitby on 2nd November 1954. Since 1934 Scarborough has been the home for a dozen different A8s at various times. No.69886 had its first taste of the Scarborough sea air in March 1945 when it was transferred from Starbeck but eighteen months later it moved to West Auckland. It was from that same depot that this A8 returned to Scarborough in June 1950 whereupon it resided for over five years, leaving for Botanic Gardens shed in Hull at the end of the summer timetable in September 1955. Normally employed on the Whitby services from Scarborough, the A8 were finally ousted from the coast route in 1959. The last three Pacific tanks allocated to Scarborough were all condemned between the end of December 1959 (69867 and 69877) and June 1960 (69885). Note Falsgrave tunnel on the left leading to Whitby via the steeply graded but now defunct coastal route.

Thompson B1 No.61176 exits Falsgrave Road tunnel on 3rd November 1954 with the 9.30 a.m. service from Middlesbrough to Scarborough. The train will shortly stop in the middle road, adjacent to Londesborough Road station, after which the B1 will run round its stock, couple up and haul the train into Central station tender first. At the end of the summer timetable in 1955, trains of no more than two coaches (basically the Scarborough-Whitby services) were given permission to propel their trains into and out of Central station without the requirement to run round. From as early as 1934 a similar procedure was permissible for trains of up to five coaches but only those trains using the newly opened platform 1A at Scarborough (Central). 1A was essentially an extension of platform 1 and was only used during the summer timetable period when Whitby line trains always exceeded two coaches but rarely more than five.

D49 Part 2 No.62769 THE OAKLEY, one of the Scarborough batch of Gresley 4-4-0s, runs into Scarborough (Central) past Londesborough Road station on 3rd November 1955. The train is the 10.29 a.m. Hull (Paragon) to Scarborough (Central) stopping at all stations. The stock appears to consist mainly of Thompson era vehicles. On the adjacent line a J72, No.69016 (out of frame), is heading off to Gallows Close goods yard with a short - three mineral wagons and a brakevan - freight. Scarborough engine shed, like many during the fifties, and all during the next decade, had a problem with cleaners, or the lack of them.

In most towns and cities in Britain back-to-back terraced housing, high rise flats or maisonettes inhabit the land adjacent to the railway near the terminus but in Scarborough some rather grandiose dwellings line the railway. Holbeck 'Jubilee' No.45619 NIGERIA is seen leaving the terminus in November 1954 with the 12.38 p.m. York job which appears to have quite a cosmopolitan selection of motive power at its head each time we see it.

It's that train again or rather its incoming working from Bradford (Forster Square) on a sunny but cold 22nd January 1955. A Holbeck Caprotti 5 has charge today, No.44757, one of seven of the type allocated to Leeds. We get a good view of Falsgrave signal box from this position, its rear wall adjacent to the Whitby line. The timber built but long deserted platform 1A also shows up nicely in this somewhat pleasing view of the Central station throat. Also appearing for the first time are the villas on the west side of the railway to back up my point about the type of housing prevalent hereabouts. It must be cold because the platelayers are wrapped up warmly; no doubt long johns are a hidden element of their attire.

Now it's really cold. It is 24th February 1955 and winter is hanging on for a few more weeks before the welcome warmth of spring creeps in slowly. In the meantime, some spectacular photography can be got by the trackside, assuming that the cold has not penetrated the cameraman's body too much to bring on the shivers. This picture seems about right as our old friend A8 No.69886 gets into its stride past Scarborough motive power depot and Gasworks signal box with the 2.45 p.m. all stations to Hull.

Another Scarborough to Hull stopping train - the 1.03 p.m. this one - heads past Falsgrave box on another cold January day in 1955, the 26th. Thompson L1 No.67763 of Hull Botanic Gardens shed is the motive power and although only six years and five days old, and just eight months out of a Heavy General overhaul including a repaint, it looks rather run down and unkempt. By June 1956, with the coming of diesel multiple units, the L1 will have been transferred away from Hull to Middlesbrough where much of the same kind of duties awaited it. The engine would of course visit Scarborough again firstly on services from Middlesbrough and later from Whitby where it spent a couple of months in early 1957. However, from thereon it was down hill all the way to the scrapyard at North Road Darlington in May 1963 via Middlesbrough again, Darlington and finally Ardsley.

Besides the *SCARBOROUGH FLYER*, which was the direct express service to King's Cross, certain other express passenger services linked Scarborough with London too, although with through coaches only. This is the 10.20 a.m. Leeds express, on Saturday 12th February 1955, which will detach two coaches for King's Cross at the York stop. Thompson B1 No.61015 DUIKER of York shed is the train engine and the graffiti on the buffer states '...3 shed, Sat...?' Platform 1A is still deserted - the summer season is still some time off - but we can see the transition point where the timber platform gives way to the solid asphalt and concrete slab structure. Note the signal which dated from 1934 when the extension was commissioned.

On Thursday 7th April 1955, Dairycoates WD 2-8-0 No.90030 is seen arriving in Scarborough with the morning pick-up from Bridlington. The goods train was routed through the tunnel to Gallows Close goods yard and, after sorting itself out at the small engine facility there (60ft turntable, coaling stage, water column and engine pit), No.90030 was detailed to leave '...when required...' back to Bridlington and Hull.

On the same morning and seen at virtually the same spot as the last train, but on a different line routing the train instead to Central station, L1 No.67763 is in charge of another passenger working this, however, is from Hull - the 8.35 a.m. semi-fast. To the right of the locomotive are two enginemen making their way from the motive power depot to the station, the white painted stairway and railings on top of the small embankment showing the authorised route to and from the engine shed. With the absence of any street lighting the 'black-out' style painted stairway would be visible on all but the darkest of nights. The vehicles in the left background of the photograph are not the trailing remnants of the Hull train but are instead coaches stabled near to Londesborough Road station. Note the three miniature signals controlling the three carriage sidings on this side of the main line.

On their way to York, B16/3 No.61467 and B1 No.61016 INYALA double-head the 10.20 a.m. Scarborough-Leeds express past Londesborough station on 7th April 1955. Both engines are York allocated, and although mechanically sound, their unkempt external appearance gives a clue as to where their home shed was situated. Gateshead shed had a similar regime in force but they had no B16s on the books.

Exiting Falsgrave tunnel and leaving behind a great cloud of steam and smoke, Ivatt 4MT No.43124 has charge of the morning pick-up goods to York on Saturday 9th April 1955. The sun is flexing its muscles and Scarborough awaits the holidaymakers, day-trippers and visitors. The 2-6-0 was one of two 'Flying Pigs' which were regular visitors (No.43122 was the other) from Dairycoates to Scarborough but they were both soon to leave Hull for pastures anew.

On 7th April 1955 Scarborough's own B16/1 No.61445 was the station pilot at Central. Note platform 1A is still meandering its way into the terminus (it was no wonder that passengers were allowed an extra three minutes to catch their trains on 1A after entering platform 1 at the barriers in the terminus). Scarborough must have been a contender for second place after the longest platform title went to Manchester's Exchange/Victoria 11 middle. Over the years some seven B16s have been allocated to Scarborough shed including the ill-fated No.925 which transferred to York in May 1940; No.61445 arrived from Neville Hill on 1st July 1951 and liked it so much the 4-6-0 decided to stay. The only way to prise it away from the resort was to condemn it on 4th July 1961 - ten years and three days later. One of its regular duties was the daily mineral working, which it performed to the end.

B16/1 No.61413 passes Londesborough Road station with a Saturday relief from Leeds on 9th April 1955. The coaching stock making up both excursion and relief trains never ceases to amaze and it makes one wonder if there was a mileage limit whereby the railways were 'allowed' to keep people cooped up in non-corridor stock with little or no toilet facilities. This formation is composed almost entirely of suburban stock, the first two vehicles being an articulated set of unknown vintage.

Deep into the summer timetable by now, its Sunday 26th June 1955, and we have another 'relief' approaching Scarborough. This train is from Hull and is headed by K3 No.61844 which is not only passing the straight road engine shed but also B1 No.61162. The Doncaster based B1 is making its way to the depot for servicing after leaving the stock of its train, an excursion from Mexborough made up with some nice Gresley corridor stock, in the Down carriage sidings. Doncaster would supply nearly all of the excursion traffic from Mexborough with motive power as Mexborough depot rarely had anything suitable amongst its large fleet of freight locomotives and tank engines. Hull on the other hand had plenty of mixed traffic and passenger locomotives at its three engine sheds suitable for the short hop to places such as Scarborough. The grotty looking No.61844 came from Dairycoates and was halfway between major overhauls so would remain in this deplorable state until March 1956.

Amongst all the passenger traffic arriving and leaving Scarborough, not to mention the associated empty carriage stock movements and the goods trains, there was usually a J72 working the local shunting duties almost as if invisible. On Saturday 18th June 1955 J72 No.69016, one of the BR built batch from January 1950, was engaged in removing mineral empties from the gasworks to Gallows Close goods yard in a manner which would hardly be described as invisible. Just two weeks old at the time of its arrival in Scarborough, the 0-6-0T had transferred from York and in doing so had made motive power history as being the first NER designed 0-6-0T to be allocated to Scarborough. In fact only two other 0-6-0Ts had ever been allocated before and they were a pair ex WD J94s, No.8016 September 1946 to May 1947 and No.68017 from September 1946 to January 1950. Our little history maker here was transferred back to York on the 21st day of December 1958 but 50A sent another J72 in its place, No.68739 but by the following August it had been condemned so another 0-6-0T was requested and received. It too came from York but was a complete 'foreigner' in the shape of ex LMS 0-6-0T No.47403 which arrived 13th September 1959 and actually ended its days at Scarborough being withdrawn on 26th September 1961. Therein ended the history of 0-6-0T engines at Scarborough.

En route to Butlins at Filey, and squeezing past the engine shed and Gasworks signal box on the 18th June 1955, B16/3 No.61448 is drawing the empty coaching stock along one of the two independent lines situated on the west side of the main lines. Another York B16/3, it is not clear if No.61448 brought in the Filey e.c.s. or if it was responsible for another inbound working and afterwards employed to haul e.c.s. from whichever Scarborough yard. One thing which was certain during the summer seasons of the 1950s - Scarborough was a busy place which required total dedication from the operating and planning staff if all was to go smooth. It usually did too!

En route to the Down carriage sidings just south of the motive power depot, BR Standard Cl.3 2-6-0 No.77004 had charge of the e.c.s. of the 8.02 a.m. train from Darlington to Scarborough and as it draws up to Gasworks signal box it appears that the 'bobby' wants a word with the Darlington crew. Barely fifteen months old, the Swindon built 2-6-0 would work the return train back to Darlington at 7.10 p.m. Altogether half of the twenty members of this class worked from NE area sheds after delivery during 1954. The engines were popular with crews not only for the quality of the ride (compared with the A8s) and the comfort of the cab but also for the lower water consumption on the Darlington-Scarborough trips for instance whereby a B1 or A8 would require a water stop at Whitby and sometimes even Loftus too for the Pacific tank, whereas the Cl.3 could manage the whole trip without having to take water thereby giving the crew the option. This particular engine, although deserting the Scarborough services of 1956 for duties on the Stainmore line, was to return by way of Whitby on both passenger and goods services.

As mentioned earlier, the Scarborough-Whitby services used platform 1A at Central station during the period of the summer timetable and here on 23rd July 1955 A8 No.69885 has a full head of steam prior to taking out the 8.12 a.m. working to Whitby. At the off the engine will simply propel its train southwards to a point where it can stop, pull forward to cross onto the track of the Whitby route and then once the whole train was clear of the Central approaches resume engine first running again. The presence of Falsgrave signal box watching over the proceedings numerous times everyday must have given the footplate crews that extra confidence for what was essentially an out of order, but nevertheless permitted manoeuvre.

Just before the A8 began its two-way journey to the north on that 23rd day of July 1955, D49/2 No.62737 THE YORK AND AINSTY reversed into the terminus in order to work the 8.28 a.m. all stations stopping train to Hull (Paragon). The nameplate of the 4-4-0 is rather clean, gleaming perhaps, compared with the rest of the engine but the Botanic Gardens 'Hunt' will soon be gleaming all over because it was due to visit Darlington works for a Heavy General overhaul within two weeks. The general activity of a busy railway terminus during the early morning is something to enjoy, even better if you can stand back and soak it all in - being neither a passenger or railway employee - and Scarborough (Central) was just the place to do so in the Fifties. Just visible in platform 1 another train is ready for departure.

Back in 1953, Thursday 26th March to be precise, D49/2 No.62756 THE BROCKLESBY was working the pilot at Central station and this nice view of platform 1 shows the 4-4-0 hauling some empty stock out of the terminus. In the shadows under the canopy it is possible to make out what may well have been the longest station seat in the world which was some 600 to 700 yards in length. Somebody, somewhere would know the precise length and also whether or not the bench could claim the world record - it would be nice to think so. During the winter period this platform serviced the Whitby trains, that canopy offering some protection from the elements.

Back to the sunshine but staying in 1953 and the spring days of May. It is the 24th of the month and D49/2 No.62701 DERBYSHIRE arrives at platform 2 with the 8.35 a.m. semi-fast from Hull, the first vehicle of which is a parcels van or full brake. Making its presence known by dint of the smoke emitting from its chimney, B1 No.61339 is brewing up prior to departing with the 10.20 a.m. Scarborough-Leeds express. The B1 was from the York allocation and would work right through to Leeds.

D11 No.62667 SOMME and an unidentified B1 pass the Down carriage sidings on the approach to Scarborough at about midday with an excursion from Mexborough on 26th July 1953. This train was destined for Londesborough Road station (opened June 1908 and known as Washbeck excursion station until renamed 1st June 1933. It closed after the last train had left on Sunday 25th August 1963) and after the passengers had detrained the two engines and their carriages would proceed through Falsgrave tunnel, and pass Gallows Close yard en route to Northstead carriage sidings alongside the Whitby line. Here the vast array of excursion carriages would assemble to await their return journey, the motive power would have been turned, serviced and coupled up to the other end to simmer away the afternoon whilst their crews took advantage of the few hours freedom afforded them - it was only a short walk to the beach. For the homeward journey the crews and their charges would leave from the carriage sidings at the appointed times for the short run to Londesborough Road station where a stop was made for just a couple of minutes prior to departure. Excursionists had to be quick in boarding the right train. These movements would save both time and congestion at the approach to Scarborough (Central).

Following the route of the excursion stock headed by the D11, Middlesbrough A8 No.69876 is seen passing Gallows Close signal box on 26th July 1953 with the 4.25 p.m. Scarborough to Whitby service. The extensive goods yard can be seen stretching into the distance beyond the bridge. Note the well cultivated vegetable patch above the retaining wall and the figure (probably a railwayman) looking towards the passing train. Permission to use the unfenced piece of embankment as an allotment would probably only be given to an employee of BR or formerly LNER, assuming of course such permission had been sought. Some interesting points of the permanent way are on display here in that stone ballast does not appear to exist and instead a mixture of ash, dirt and fine stone constitute the track bed - modellers take note.

SCARBOROUGH Departures - Sunday 27th July 1952: Observations from 6.00 pm.

Time	Reporting No.	To	Motive Power
P.M.			
6.00	—	Hull	61215
6.30	—	York rlf	62739
6.40‡	373	Moorthorpe ret exc	60905
6.50	96	Newcastle ret exc	61422
7.00	—	York	44665
7.10‡	213	Castleford ret exc	61411
7.20‡	376	Bolton on Dearne ret exc	61037
7.27	—	York	61454
7.55	—	Leeds	61465
8.02	282	Goole ret exc	61080
8.10	—	Leeds	62769
8.27‡	283	Hull ret exc	61305
8.33	211	Selby ret exc	61035
8.40	—	Hull	62748
8.46‡	261	Tadcaster ret exc	61062
8.55	834	Wadsley Bridge ret exc dup	61464
9.00‡	871	Guiseley ret exc	61338
9.10‡	269	Leeds ret exc (Q)	61446
9.20‡	268	Leeds ret exc	61319
9.30	365	Wadsley Bridge ret exc	61154
9.40	881	Chesterfield Mid. ret exc	44672
9.50	366	Mexborough ret exc	61120
10.00	835	Mexborough ret exc #	61128

Notes:

All times are scheduled not actual.

rlf	relief.
addl	additional.
ret exc	return excursion.
dup	duplicate.
Q	runs if required.
#	duplicate to 366.
‡	Londesborough Road station.

Gallows Close again but looking northwards this time as the 9.30 a.m. Middlesbrough to Scarborough train ambles along towards is destination behind A8 No.69880 on 24th May 1953. Two unidentified tank engines, both partly hidden by the signal gantry, shunt the goods yard in that continuous to-ing and fro-ing manner which is now, sadly, no longer part of the British railway scene.

A general view of Central station in October 1954 with departures imminent. The townscape of Scarborough looms above the platform canopies as if watching the activity which by now would be somewhat lessened from the frenzied comings and goings of the summer months.

Observed by a young man who could barely see over the wall, a London Midland Region 'Crab' No.42763 arrives in Scarborough on 11th July 1953 with a holiday extra from Sheffield (Midland) - M236. It least the coaching stock making up the formation appears to be of reasonable quality corridor coaches. Approaching platform 1, the 2-6-0 has another interested party running alongside on platform 1A - he'll never be able to race it to the buffers, will he? Note the polished stonework where countless backsides have sat patiently waiting for the various arrivals over the years hoping, and often getting, the odd gem from miles away.

SCARBOROUGH Departures - Easter Monday, 30th March 1959: Observations post 3.00 pm.

Time	Reporting No.	To	Motive Power
P.M.			
3.05	476	King's Cross rlf	60864
3.20	n/a	York	61434
4.00	217	York rlf	61418
4.19	n/a	Bradford	73169
4.40	n/a	Hull	DMU
5.55	218	York rlf	61036
6.15	262	Leeds ret exc	61035
6.20	282	Hull rlf	61305
6.25‡	572	Huddersfield ret exc	73165
6.30	n/a	Hull	DMU
6.45	219	Leeds rlf	61438
6.55	218A	York dup rlf	61467
7.00‡	550	Bradford Exchange ret exc	61274
7.10	344	Bolton on Dearne ret exc	61839
7.20‡	589	Marsden ret exc	44845
7.30	264	Kippax ret exc	61016
7.50	220	Leeds rlf	73167
8.00	n/a	Leeds	61259
8.30	555	Batley ret exc	61110
8.35‡	281	Hull ret exc	61289
8.50‡	340	Heeley ret exc	73155
9.00	552	Bradford ret exc	61309
9.20	265	Leeds ret exc	61266
9.30	556	Wakefield ret exc	61013
9.40	554	Laisterdyke ret exc	61123
9.50	266	Leeds ret exc	61455

Notes:

All times are scheduled not actual.

rlf relief.
dup duplicate.
ret exc return excursion.
‡ Londesborough Road station.
n/a Not applicable - Ordinary passenger working.

N.B. Note complete absence of Class B16/1 except 61445 on Station Pilot duty with 82026.
All the D49's were in store at this time.

Goodbye holidaymakers. B1 No.61115 departs from Central station on 25th July 1953 with the 12.05 p.m. holiday train for Kings Norton. Note the train has yet to find the metals of the up fast but the next signal and points should put it exactly onto the correct route. The timing of this train allows us to observe the goings-on at platform 1A where an A8 waits at the buffer stops as the stock from a Whitby arrival disgorges its passengers. The locomotive which worked the train from Whitby is still at the head (south) end waiting to uncouple and make its way to the shed. Once the train is empty the nearest A8 would buffer up to the stock and await prospective passengers for the Whitby line. At departure the A8 would reverse and propel the stock far enough past the Whitby line junction to gain access.

Having already found their route and starting to make smoke now, a D20 No.62378 and D49/2 No.62748 THE SOUTHWOLD approach Gasworks signal box with an afternoon train for York on 17th July 1953; the train consists of just six vehicles including two four-wheeled vans, two bogie brakes and two passenger coaches which appear to be suburban stock. Four lines of empty coaches, for later booked return excursions, can be seen in the Up carriage siding. Over on the locomotive yard only one engine is visible but the two lines of coal wagons for feeding the stage and storing the empties, are plain to see, as is the inclination of the ramp. Note the gentleman on the right side of the fence with his galvanised bucket. His attire would probably be his regular clothes throughout the year, no matter what the weather.

THE SCARBOROUGH FLYER headed by D49/2 No.62769 THE OAKLEY, but minus suitable headboard, departs Scarborough for King's Cross on Sunday 2nd August 1953 at the appointed time. En route the train will stop at Malton to pick-up two coaches from Whitby. At York the 4-4-0 will come off to be replaced by a V2 or even a Pacific and a headboard will magically appear on the engine. For some unexplained reason the North Eastern Region, and its forefathers, did not like locomotive headboards but at least they were not adverse to the carriage stock having roof boards. However, York shed could not be bothered for the most part with fixing the headboard from 1953 onwards anyway on the York-Scarborough section of the train's journey. So, the decline could be said to have accelerated then and by the end of the 1962 summer timetable the train no longer existed - at least in name. The 'Flyer' did not have a long history in railway terms and being only a summer period express it did not have the same clout as those named trains carrying businessmen throughout the year for instance. The history was certainly interesting to the observer, and perhaps a little complicated, not least of which was the headboard itself which first appeared in the summer of 1932 as *SCARBOROUGH FLIER* on two lines; next came the same name but on one line for the York to Scarborough portion of the journey. The Second World War put paid to named trains but when BR resumed their use and the reintroduced 'Flyer' now carried a prefix and a change in spelling - *THE SCARBOROUGH FLYER* over two lines on the headboard. In 1952 a new standardised headboard was introduced on BR and the post-war wording was split over three lines on a cast metal board. The final, and perhaps the most ambitious headboard was introduced in 1959 and though it was a standard board with three lines of lettering as before, it had the addition of a sun and rays projecting there from at each of the top corners. At least six people, most of whom are not enthusiasts, but are most probably out for a Sunday stroll, are looking over the wall at the spectacle of the D49 and its already heavy train blasting its way out of town.

18th July 1953 - the 10.00 a.m. Scarborough (Londesborough Road) to Manchester (London Road) [242] heads out of town with B1 No.61257 appearing to be making light work of the ten-coach load as it passes an inbound train at Gasworks box. Where the Neville Hill B1 worked this train too is unknown because it could have taken two obvious routes through the Pennines. The most likely would have been via Sheffield and Woodhead whilst Leeds, Huddersfield, Stalybridge and Guide Bridge also springs to mind but this latter route, missing out the last junction station, would more likely have taken the train into Manchester (Victoria) or even (Exchange). So, the Woodhead line seems to have been the most likely. Whichever way was eventually taken by the train, it would have been an interesting journey.

Another interesting journey in the making on Saturday 18th July 1953. V2 No.60909 departs Scarborough with the 1.00 p.m. holiday express [302] for Glasgow (Queen Street) due at 8.04 p.m. This train occupied platforms 8 and 9 (four coaches each) and the whole train departed from No.9. Running as far as Malton, a pilot would be picked up there and attached to the rear of the train. The train would then reverse back to Scarborough to reach the line for Driffield and once clear of the junction train engine No.60909 would proceed onto the Gilling line and reach the East Coast Main Line at Pilmoor. Thereafter train 302 was clear all the way to its destination.

SCARBOROUGH Departures - Whit Monday 1960: Observation from 3.53 pm.

Time	Reporting No.	To	Motive Power
P.M.			
3.53	905	Sheffield Midland rlf	61218
5.05*	341	Sheffield Midland ret exc	73171
5.15	280	Leeds rlf	61237
5.24	262	Leeds ret exc	61259
5.34	212	Castleford ret exc	60879
5.40*	345	Heath ret exc	61964
5.45	263	Leeds ret exc	61414
6.10	283	Hull rlf	61927
6.17*	551	Batley ret exc	61023
6.25	550	Bradford Exchange ret exc	61295
6.30*	218A	York (control ordered) rlf	61434
6.37	279	Leeds rlf	61415
6.50	208	Heeley (c.o.) rlf ret exc	44249
6.55	M992	King's Norton ret exc	44888
7.00*	340	Heeley ret exc	44082
7.05	222	Filey ecs (ret exc to York)	61069
7.10	261	Leeds ret exc	61429
7.25*	282	Hull rlf	61813
7.30	220	Normanton rlf	60831
7.40	554	Stanningley ret exc	61013
7.45*	351	Retford ret exc	61225
7.50	223	Leeds rlf	61432
8.00	224	Leeds	61447
8.10*	281	Hull ret exc	61847
8.18*	337	Barnsley Exchange ret exc	61828
8.37*	352	Doncaster ret exc	61868
8.45	232	York rlf	61468
8.55	968	Featherstone ret exc	61975
9.23	270	Leeds ret exc	61471
9.43	271	Leeds ret exc	61435
9.53	272	Leeds ret exc	61448
10.03*	362	Bolton on Dearne ret exc	61883
10.13	970	Halifax ret exc	61039

Notes: All times are scheduled not actual.
rlf relief.
ret exc return excursion.
c.o. control ordered.
* Start from Londesborough Road station - e.c.s. to and from Gallows Close but not Nos.351 and 281.

Scarborough Station Pilots: 62739, 62762, 82026.

'Jubilee' No.45659 DRAKE gets into its stride passing the Up carriage sidings outside Central with an afternoon train to York on 19th November 1954.

It is early May 1955 and time for all those excursionists to leave their mundane post-war lives back at home and enjoy a day at the seaside. Thompson B1 No.61166 negotiates the pointwork - whilst the carriages behind seem to want to go their own way - outside Central station as it approaches with a train from Mexborough. The 4-6-0 is one of Mexborough's own; hence the all round shine.

One of the Saturday morning departures from Scarborough in 1955, albeit empty carriage stock, was the working to Filey to pick up passengers from Butlin's Holiday Camp. Entrusted with that duty on 23rd July was B16/3 No.61420, another York engine but one which was only a few weeks out of the shops from a heavy overhaul and therefore very clean! This engine had arrived earlier in the morning from 50A in order to work this particular turn.

Here we have *THE SCARBOROUGH FLYER* complete with headboard and a B16/3, No.61472, accelerating out of town on the Saturday working of 23rd July 1955. Besides the headboard, the reporting number 308 is also displayed. I suppose it was all down to who was in charge on the day. Next stop Malton!

After the rostered Scarborough D49 failed, a B16/1, No.61445, substituted as motive power for the 8.07 a.m. Leeds express on 27th March 1956. With departure from Central imminent, the 4-6-0 is wreathed in its own steam produced by the chilly conditions.

On that same day, 27th March 1956, the 8.15 a.m. Scarborough to Hull express was made up of the British Railways Mark 1 coaching stock and here shortly after departure time Dairycoates B1 No.61065 blasts away from Central in anticipation of a clear run to Paragon. The No.1A platform is quiet at this time but employment would not be far away.

The 10.00 a.m. Scarborough (Londesborough Road) to Manchester (London Road) passes Gasworks box on the morning of 23rd July 1955 - the day was ideal for photography as well as train watching - with York B16/2 No.61475 in charge. This little corner of Scarborough was a favourite with spotters' with a couple of elevated viewpoints, courtesy of the gasworks wall, to give different aspects of the passing traffic. Looking at the length of the trains and the frequency it makes you realise how much personal travel modes and tastes have changed over the intervening years from a period which must have been the heyday of the BR excursion era.

Coming into Scarborough later that morning is B16/1 No.61422 with the 8.50 a.m. from Normanton. Already heads are out of the carriage windows as the passengers anticipate the delights in store for them at the fast approaching seaside. Local enthusiasts' bicycles line the fence in growing numbers as the parade of arrivals mounts to a crescendo at about midday.

The details concerning the exact time, date and train is lost for this picture but it shows B1 No.61267 in mid summer with train [364], approaching Scarborough in pouring rain, and 'pegged' it seems, for a platform at Central station. However, one certainty is the track leading in from the right which came from the north opening of the roundhouse and would have been used by tank engines going through servicing.

(top) In order to gain access to the Up main from the engine shed, York B1 No.61084 propels two D20s, Nos.62349 and 62392, towards Washbeck signal box on Sunday 7th June 1953. The 4-4-0s, both in light steam, were being transferred from a rather long winter storage at Scarborough back into traffic. No.62349 was en route to York thence to Gateshead after being transferred (on paper) from its 1952 home at Alnmouth. The other D20 was also en route to York but from there it would make its own way to its official residence at Selby. After the short summer period of working this latter engine would again enter storage from which it did not return in 1954 and was instead condemned in May. (below) Having gained the main line the trio head west past Gasworks signal box and the gated rail entrance to the local gasworks.

B1 No.61224 approaches Scarborough on Saturday 23rd July 1955 with the morning 'slow' from York - generally called the parcels - which is routed for Central station where it would fit nicely into one of the shorter platforms. Note the gated line leading to the gasworks on the left, with its attendant row of empty mineral wagons waiting for a Monday morning pick-up. Remember that barred fencing? As a youngster it was the ideal place to park your backside whilst you enjoyed the ever changing spectacle of the passing trains. Wherever you may have watched the trains, in upper or lower quadrant country, once that signal was pegged your senses picked up. First the hearing went into top gear, then the eyes went into virtual strain mode and finally expectation, and excitement worked together to lift you well above the fence line before crashing back down to earth as one of the local tank engines came into sight. But there was always another signal coming off and the whole wonderful experience would start again!

On 2nd July 1955, D49/1 No.62722 HUNTINGDONSHIRE brings a heavy 9.00 a.m. Hull train into Scarborough. Framed beneath the gantry which effectively joined the gasworks with the motive power depot, the 4-4-0 appears to be taking to its task effortlessly. Old and young observe its progress. Note the ladders used by some intrepid soul to capture a better picture on film than they did last time! This one seems pretty good to me.

SCARBOROUGH'S ENGINE SHEDS AND THE MOTIVE POWER:

The roundhouse at Scarborough engine shed dated from 1882 and had replaced a small two-road shed which had stood on the site of what became Londesborough Road excursion station and had been built in 1845 by the York & North Midland Railway. In what was to be a trebling of stabling space, the North Eastern Railway added an eight-road dead-end shed in 1890 and this facility was built further down the yard, south of the existing roundhouse. Besides the typical NER style coal stage, the depot eventually got a 60ft turntable to supplement the 44ft example in the roundhouse. In late 1955 half of the straight shed roof, and its supporting walls on the eastern side of the building, was taken down over four of the stabling roads and the shed remained in that condition up to closure on Saturday 20th July 1963.

A servicing facility consisting 60ft turntable, coaling crane, stage, engine pit and water tank, was opened by the NER at Gallows Gate in 1908 to cater for the locomotives running in on excursion traffic. This facility closed at the end of the summer season of 1958 and from thereon visiting locomotives had to use the main shed at Seamer Road. A similar locomotive servicing area was provided at Northstead carriage sidings so that line occupation between that facility and Seamer Road shed was kept to a minimum.

During the British Railways period up to the end of 1960, the number of locomotives allocated to Scarborough motive power depot ranged on average from ten to fourteen engines at any one time, with tank and tender engines being present, roughly, in equal numbers. Seasonal vagaries saw all sorts of different locomotive types come and go, many new to East Yorkshire.

The former NER Atlantic's had all gone from the shed by the end of 1948, replaced, in the main, by LNER D49s. Goods engines had never been at the top of the depot's 'list of requirements', but in 1949 three J39s arrived to bolster the stud. However, the J39s were useful engines and were equally happy on either goods or passenger working. 1950 saw two of the J39s move on, their place taken by a solitary, but new, Ivatt LMS design 4MT 2-6-0; that engine left the shed in July of the following year. In the January of 1950 the establishment received its first ever J72 class 0-6-0 tank engine, and a nearly new one at that in the shape of BR built No.69016. That particular engine remained at Scarborough until the end of December 1958 when it was replaced by another of its ilk, No.68739. The J72 had replaced J94 68017, one of a pair which had arrived in Scarborough during the LNER period. The large Class A8 Pacific tanks had long been associated with Scarborough and during the early 50s they remained a 'constant' at the shed with up to five of them 'on the books' by 1955. In the interim period another ex LMS design, 2-6-4T No.42083, had infiltrated the allocation but only for a month in the summer of 1952. LMS engines were no strangers to Scarborough and many of them had worked into the seaside town on excursions from far and wide since Grouping but to have one actually stationed permanently seemed to have a chill of something sinister in the offing.

During 1953 and 1954 none of the Scarborough engines left the shed for greener pastures, or otherwise, but during the same period two D49s came aboard. On the first day of 1955 the allocation of Scarborough shed stood at fourteen locomotives consisting a solitary B16 (one of a pair which came to the shed in 1951), seven 'Hunts/Shires', five A8s and one J72. The figures for 1955 were not those of the heady days at Grouping when no less than twenty-seven North Eastern engines graced the stabling roads of the shed, they were though up from the end of 1947 when eleven engines made up the allocation. However, from the end of the Summer Timetable of 1955 things started changing and not for the better. Sunday, 25th September brought two BR built, LMS 2-6-4 tank engines in exchange for two A8s.

In 1956 two more A8s left but nothing took their place. During that year the LMS designed 2-6-4Ts could not make their minds up to stay or not; in the end they did, for a couple of years anyway. To add insult, perhaps, to the remains of the LNER stud, two BR Standard 2-6-4 tank engines arrived at the shed in February but moved away in May. Nothing changed in 1957 until mid-June when two familiar A8s, 69881 and 69885, came back; the latter left again in September. The end of the year saw another familiar stalwart leave when D49 No.62726 went off for scrapping. The year 1958 could be described, at least within the confines of Scarborough engine shed, as a 'balancing year'. The two 'foreigners' with funny numbers, 42084 and 42085, moved away in June to be replaced by two A8s - nice, but another A8 had been condemned along with three D49s. Replacements consisted two D49s and two BR Standard 2-6-2Ts, 82028 and 82029! In December the faithful J72 was swapped for another 0-6-0T. So 1958 was seven in, seven out - status quo.

On 25th January 1959 four of BR's finest Standard Class 5s arrived to take over everything, or so it seemed but they had all returned from whence they came by the middle of June. During the short stay of the Standard 5s, three of the depot's remaining D49s were withdrawn but to save the day three Thompson B1s arrived in the nick of time. August was not a good month for the lone J72, after less than a year at the seaside it was condemned. In September some would say that things took another turn for the worse when ex LMS 0-6-0T No.47403 was plonked onto the allocation. The final arrival of the year and which was no stranger to Scarborough, was BR Standard Cl.3 2-6-0 No.77004 shortly after Bonfire Night. But, the year was not yet finished and in the penultimate week of December another A8 was condemned followed seven days later by yet another. The tally for the year, not including the 'short stayers' was five engines in, and six out.

The change of decade did not change the depot's fortunes and March 1960 saw the three B1s move away but, more significantly, the two D49s and the remaining A8 were condemned. J39 No.64904 came in September but moved on the following month. Only B16 No.61445 remained as the sole LNER representative. Two more BR Standard 2-6-2 tank engines came in June and by October another BR Standard 2-6-0 had arrived. So 1960 saw three engines in but six leaving. 1961 saw one new arrival, a Stanier 2-6-2T looking for work which did not exist. Two of the BR Standard tanks left, the LMS 0-6-0T was withdrawn and the last LNER engine, B16 No.61445 was condemned. One in - four out.

Why the depot remained open, maintaining just five locomotives, into 1962 is a mystery. Perhaps the summer excursion traffic and its empty stock movements required the presence of the tank engines. By now diesel multiple units had taken over the local services to Hull and Bridlington, so the engine shed soldiered on - just. One of the Ivatt designed LMS Cl.2 2-6-0s, No.46409, arrived in January and hung around until October doing what little work there was but mainly spending long periods in store. The end of the year found the Stanier tank officially condemned. The two remaining Standard tanks left separately in December leaving the two Standard 2-6-0s.

Miraculously Scarborough engine shed welcomed in the New Year of 1963 but closed officially on 20th July after one of the coldest winters of the 20th Century. Of the two BR Standards still hanging around, No.77013 left on Monday 25th February for an overhaul at Crewe works and never returned whilst No.77004 went to York shed on 9th April. York then sent another BR Standard, 2-6-2 tank No.82027 in its place 'on loan' to clear up, clear out the stored engines and clear off on the 18th May 1963 with the last two, Nos.40117 and 41265, the latter having been dumped at Scarborough since its withdrawal at Malton shed in the previous December.

The last year of the shed's life saw some interesting 'boarders' arrive and depart. Displaced by English Electric Type 4 diesels at York depot, five V2s arrived at Scarborough in April 1962 - 60831, 60837, 60847, 60864 and 60877 did little or no work and returned en masse to York in mid-October. Before their departure, however, four Thompson and one of Peppercorn's A2 Pacifics, complete with nameplates, arrived from York for storage in September followed by another of their kind in October; their numbers were: 60515, 60516, 60518, 60522, 60526 and 60512 respectively. The departure of the 4-6-2s was spasmodic with No.60518 being towed away on 29th November 1962 for scrap. On 12th December Nos.60512 and 60522 were moved out and transferred for further work in Scotland. On 9th March 1963 the sole Peppercorn A2 member of the sextet, 60526, went away in steam, even though it had been withdrawn during the previous December. The next day found the last two 'celebs', 60515 and 60516 being towed off on their journey to Doncaster for cutting up.

So, to sum up, Scarborough was never a shed with a large locomotive allocation, nor were its engines deemed to be the creme de la creme of the motive power world. More likely they could be better described as 'hand me downs' or 'second-hand' but, nevertheless the stud was interesting, even up to closure. Without a doubt, each summer season brought the place to life and out of its long winter slumber. For five months each year and without the benefit of modern appliances such as coaling and ash plants, the depot cared for, on a daily basis, locomotives from all over the country. Getting the trains, with their hordes of day excursionists, and sometimes 'foreign' motive power away from Scarborough 'on time' was something that Scarborough shed seemed to specialise in.

(below) During what appears to be a quieter moment near the motive power depot on 2nd July 1955, one of Scarborough's own D49/2, No.62756 THE BROCKLESBY, makes its way along the independent line to the Down carriage siding with stock from an earlier arrival at Central. The high pitched roofs of the roundhouse, with the myriad of glazing, forms a backdrop for the signal gantries in view.

With the ever present local gasworks forming the background, we have a busy summer Sunday afternoon at Scarborough shed before us on 7th June 1953, as a Stanier Cl.5 arrives on the stabling yard from servicing to join the mixed bag of visiting engines. Note that virtually all the locomotives are facing west ready for their homeward journey. Amongst the few exceptions are a couple of A8 tanks ready for duties on the Whitby route. In late 1955 subsidence caused the left hand section of the shed, covering the four roads nearest the main line, to be demolished as being unsafe - even for locomotive use - although the open-air tracks were still employed for stabling. Of the tender engines on show, there are B16, B1 and K3 classes, plus whatever was inside the shed.

This was the view from the fence on Seamer Road above the motive power depot. It is 30th April 1955 and D49/2 No.62739 THE BADWORTH is going well as it sets out from Scarborough with the 2.45 p.m. 'stopper' to Hull. In sidings alongside the coaling stage ramp, reserved for the stabling of mineral wagons, a bolster wagon with what appears to be old rail for cargo and a couple of opens' with newly cut timber, share with the empty and full coal wagons. Was some building work imminent?

The locomotive allocation of Scarborough engine shed from 1st January 1923 to closure.

The origin of subsequent transfers to Scarborough is given in the secind column of the table whilst subsequent transfers away from Scarborough are given in the fourth column.

A6

No.	From	Dates	To
688 / 9792	Malton	4/6/41-12/3/45	Starbeck.
689 / 69793	Whitby	22/8/34-12/3/45	Starbeck.
691 / 69795	Malton	6/10/41-12/3/45	Starbeck.
693 / 69797	Resident	1/1/23-27/6/34	Whitby.
694 / 69798	Starbeck	by 1/12/23-17/5/35	Hull B.G.
	Hull B.G	30/5/35-5/8/40	Malton.

A8

No.	From	Dates	To
2160 / 69867	Selby	1/7/51-21/10/51	Selby.
	Selby	8/6/52-9/1/55	Hull B.G.
	Hull B.G.	29/5/55-23/12/59c	Scrap.
1520 / 69873	Nev. Hill	22/5/35-2/12/35	Hull B.G.
1529 / 69876	Heaton	29/5/34-16/10/34	Starbeck.
1531 / 69877	Hull B.G.	4/6/50-19/11/50	Selby.
	Nev. Hill	8/4/58-30/12/59c	Scrap.
1500 / 69879	Selby	1/7/51-25/9/55	Hull B.G.
1502 / 69881	Heaton	6/6/36-26/2/40	Starbeck.
	Starbeck	12/3/45-9/1/55	Hull B.G.
	Hull B.G.	29/5/55-9/12/56	Nev. Hill.
	Nev. Hill	16/6/57-2/6/58c	Scrap.
1503 / 69882	Saltburn	17/7/49-1/10/50	Whitby.
1526 / 69885	H1 reb.	20/5/36-6/10/41	Selby.
	Selby	12/3/45-21/10/51	Selby.
	Selby	8/6/52-9/12/56	Nev. Hill.
	Nev. Hill	16/6/57-15/9/57	Nev. Hill.
	Nev. Hill	8/6/58-20/6/60c	Scrap.
1527 / 69886	Starbeck	12/3/45-29/9/46	W. Auck.
	W. Auck.	4/6/50-25/9/55	Hull B.G.
1329 / 69888	Heaton	29/5/34-6/11/34	Heaton.
1326 / 69892	Nev. Hill	12/3/35-9/8/40	Starbeck.
1530 / 69894	Selby	12/3/45-4/6/50	Hull B.G.

B1

No.	From	Dates	To
61068	Hull B.G.	14/6/59-27/3/60	Darlton.
61304	Hull B.G.	14/6/59-27/3/60	Darlton.
61305	Hull B.G.	14/6/59-20/3/60	Hull Dy.

B15

No.	From	Dates	To
813	Resident	1/1/23-?/1/24	York.

B16

No.	From	Dates	To
908 / 61411	York	3/10/29-2/11/29	York.
923 / 61419	York	14/5/28-3/10/29	York.
925	Hull Dy.	1/6/39-25/5/40	York.
942 / 61432	York	6/7/25-28/9/25	York.
2374 / 61445	Nev. Hill	1/7/51-4/7/61c	Scrap.
2380 / 61451	Nev. Hill	4/11/51-17/2/52	York.
845 / 61474	York	15/7/24-1/10/24	York.
	York	14/1/30-28/3/43	York.

C6

No.	From	Dates	To
532	York	23/6/39-11/3/40	York.
649	York	5/6/39-11/3/40	York.
698 / 2941	York	6/7/39-11/3/40	York.
699	Gateshd.	30/5/39-3/2/40	Darlton.
701	York	5/6/39-11/3/40	York.
704 / 2947	Gateshd.	31/5/39-11/3/40	York.

C7

No.	From	Dates	To
706	York	12/3/45-21/12/46c	Scrap.
716 / 2954	Heaton	9/3/47-26/6/48c	Scrap.
720 / 2958	York	12/3/45-29/9/46	Hull Dy.
722 / 2960	York	30/12/46-8/3/47c	Scrap.
728	York	12/3/45-17/11/45c	Scrap.
729	York	12/3/45-17/11/45c	Scrap.
732 / 2963	York	12/3/45-14/12/46c	Scrap.
737	York	12/3/45-22/12/45c	Scrap.
2166 / 2972	York	26/11/45-30/8/48c	Scrap.
2167 / 2973	Heaton	9/3/47-26/6/48c	Scrap.
2169 / 2975	York	23/12/46-10/7/48c	Scrap.
2204 / 2989	York	26/11/45-30/8/48c	Scrap.
2207 / 2992	Hull Dy.	5/3/45-1/11/48c	Scrap.
2208 / 2993	York	26/11/45-6/3/48c	Scrap.
2211 / 2996	Hull Dy.	5/3/45-29/9/46	Heaton.

D17/2

No.	From	Dates	To
1874	Resident	1/1/23-18/11/32	Stockton.
1878	Resident	1/1/23-2/2/34c	Scrap.
1902 / 2112	Resident	1/1/23-19/11/34	Selby.
	Selby	5/7/37-9/1/43	Nev. Hill.
1903	Resident	1/1/23-22/3/33	Starbeck.
1906	Resident	1/1/23-29/9/34	W. Hart.
1907	Resident	1/1/23-25/9/34	W. Hart.
1928	Gateshd	11/7/25-26/8/25	Gateshd.
1929	Selby	5/7/37-20/12/37	Starbeck.
1930	W. Hart.	9/7/25-9/10/25	W. Hart.

D20

No.	From	Dates	To
2011 / 62340	Nev. Hill	26/11/40-12/3/45	Selby.
2013 / 62342	Nev. Hill	19/4/24-11/2/35	Selby.
2017	York	12/12/42-2/12/44c	Scrap.
2018 / 62347	York	29/11/40-12/3/45	Selby.
2019 / 62348	Nev. Hill	26/11/40-12/3/45	Selby.
2021 / 2350	York	28/11/40-12/3/45	Selby.
2024 / 62353	Hull B.G.	29/11/34-1/7/35	Hull B.G.
2108 / 2367	Nev. Hill	30/11/40-15/10/42	Hull B.G.
2109	Selby	5/3/42-15/10/42	Hull B.G.
708 / 62373	York	19/4/24-20/5/40	York.
711 / 62374	York	5/7/37-28/3/38	Selby.
712 / 62375	York	7/2/30-14/9/34	Starbeck.
723 / 2377	Tweed.	9/7/25-1/10/25	Tweed.
724 / 62378	York	19/4/24-17/8/40	Selby.
725 / 62379	Nev. Hill	21/1/26-13/8/34	Selby.
	Selby	11/2/35-20/5/40	York.
1147	Gateshd	9/7/30-13/8/34	Selby.
	Selby	19/11/34-19/6/39	W. Hart.

D20 class cont./

1206	Gateshd	11/7/30-30/9/35	Starbeck.
D22			
42	Hull B.G.	22/10/25-22/5/30c	Scrap.
779	Resident	1/1/23-4/2/30c	Scrap.
356	Resident	1/1/23-21/2/29	Hull B.G.
1537	Selby	14/5/25-6/7/25	Selby.
1538	Hull Sp.	?/?/24-23/6/33c	Scrap.
1541	Resident	1/1/23-9/10/25	Starbeck.
1542	Resident	1/1/23-22/2/30	Stockton.
D23			
217	Resident	1/1/23-?/?/24	Malton.
472	Resident	1/1/23-?/?/24	Nev. Hill.
1107	Resident	1/1/23-29/8/24	Hull B.G.
D49			
318 / 62720	Hull B.G.	15/10/42-2/6/43	Hull B.G.
352 / 62726	York	3/10/53-18/12/57c	Scrap.
336 / 62727	Hull B.G.	15/10/42-12/3/45	Nev. Hill.
2756 / 62731	York	6/7/52-14/9/52	Pickering.
2760 / 62735	York	11/4/54-25/8/58c	Scrap.
232 / 62739	Nev. Hill	1/7/51-11/10/60c	Scrap.
282 / 62745	York	17/8/58-16/3/59c	Scrap.
283 / 62746	Nev. Hill	15/5/48-29/5/48	Nev. Hill.
297 / 62749	Gateshd	15/8/48-25/9/49	Starbeck.
205 / 62751	York	13/6/48-13/3/59c	Scrap.
222 / 62754	New	20/7/34-29/11/34	Hull B.G.
	Hull B.G.	1/7/35-28/11/40	York.
226 / 62755	New	23/7/34-27/11/40	York.
	York	13/6/48-27/11/49	Starbeck.
230 / 62756	Nev. Hill	1/7/51-30/4/58c	Scrap.
258 / 62758	New	22/8/34-31/5/39	York
274 / 62759	New	28/8/34-26/11/40	York.
	York	2/6/43-12/3/45	York.
279 / 62760	New	3/9/34-27/11/40	York.
353 / 62761	New	12/9/34-27/11/40	York.
357 / 62762	Starbeck	8/6/58-13/10/60c	Scrap.
361 / 62764	Gateshd	11/9/49-1/7/51	Nev. Hill.
366 / 62769	Nev. Hill	29/5/48-12/9/58c	Scrap.
368 / 62770	Nev. Hill	27/7/48-14/6/59	Selby.
376 / 62774	Nev. Hill	27/4/48-15/5/48	Nev. Hill.
	Nev. Hill	15/8/48-26/9/48	Pickering.
E5			
1466	Resident	1/1/23- by 1/7/24	York.
1471	Resident	1/1/23- by 1/7/24	Selby.
F8			
262	Cudwh	17/3/29-2/11/29	Malton.
1581	Malton	?/7/24-14/5/28	York.
G5			
1701 / 67243	Resident	1/1/23-7/3/28	Hull B.G.
1883 / 67281	S. Blyth	1/1/24-?/2/25	Nev. Hill.
1886 / 67284	Heaton	6/8/27-5/7/37	Malton.
1775 / 67308	Starbeck	20/7/25-9/10/25	Starbeck.
381 / 67330	Resident	1/1/23-14/5/28	York.

G5 class cont./

580 / 67334	Nev. Hill	13/7/27-12/10/27	Nev. Hill.
149 / 67338	Starbeck	9/1/43-7/8/43	Middsbr.
G6			
951	Malton	?/12/25-22/9/26c	Scrap.
273	Carlisle	by 6/12/33-?/9/24	S. Blyth.
60	S. Blyth	20/7/25-28/9/25	S. Blyth.
343	Middsbr.	?/7/24-?/9/24	Saltburn.
87	Resident	1/1/23-?/?/24	York.
	S. Blyth	20/7/25- by 12/25	S. Blyth.
J21			
1516 / 5046	York	9/10/34-13/5/37	Hull Dy.
976	Malton	28/3/43-12/3/45	York.
582 / 5059	Darlton.	30/6/39-12/3/45	York.
1573 / 5096	York	4/7/38-5/8/40	York.
1574 / 65097	Middsbr.	28/3/43-12/3/45	Nev. Hill.
J22			
497	Resident	1/1/23-24/11/24c	Scrap.
682	Resident	1/1/23-21/12/27c	Scrap.
812	Malton	?/12/27-26/4/29c	Scrap.
1141	Resident	1/1/23-20/8/26c	Scrap.
422	Hull Dy.	?/11/24-?/1/25	Tweed.
J23			
2474	Hull Sp.	14/7/30-31/7/37c	Scrap.
2515	York	14/5/28-3/11/29	Malton.
J24			
1823 / 5602	York	15/7/35-7/10/39	Bor Gdn.
1826 / 5604	W. Hart.	26/4/39-8/5/39	Malton.
J25			
1992 / 65666	N.Blyth	4/5/28-15/7/35	York.
2129	Resident	1/1/23-12/3/27	Shildon.
2136 / 5722	Resident	1/1/23- by 1/7/24	Darlton.
J26			
1200 / 65765	York	17/10/27-2/6/39	Hull Dy.
J27			
2354 / 65876	York	6/5/42-28/3/43	N. Blyth.
J39			
1460 / 64861	Starbeck	25/9/49-23/7/50	Starbeck.
3000 / 64904	Hull Dy.	11/9/60-9/10/60	Hull Dy.
1540 / 64919	Starbeck	25/9/49-1/10/50	Nev. Hill.
1535 / 64935	Starbeck	25/9/49-7/1/51	Nev. Hill.
J72			
2332 / 68739	York	21/12/58-24/8/59c	Scrap.
69016	York	22/1/50-21/12/58	York.
J94			
8016 / 68016	York	29/9/46-25/5/47	Sunland.
8017 / 68017	York	29/9/46-22/1/50	York.
Q5			
1149 / 3297	Resident	1/1/23-15/7/24	York.
	York	1/10/24-17/2/25	Selby.
Q6			
2228 / 63385	Selby	17/2/25-6/7/25	York.
	York	4/1/26-14/5/28	York.

Y1

119 / E8143	Selby	16/4/38-30/1/39	Selby.
187 / 68151	New	1/8/29-3/6/30	Bridlington.

Y3

196 / 68159	New	23/8/29-19/2/32	Shildon.
198 / 8161	Donc.	3/6/30-16/4/38	Selby.

SENTINEL RAILCARS:

220	New	24/11/32-7/9/40c	Scrap.
246	New	6/12/32-10/9/33	Whitby.
248	New	13/12/32-9/7/33	Yar. B.
	Yar. B.	1/10/33-11/10/33	Whitby.
2136	Richmd.	7/7/34-6/11/34	Selby.
2231	Stockton	1/7/39-5/10/39	Stockton.

LMS Cl.3. 2-6-2T.

40117	Wakefd.	31/12/61-19/11/62c	Scrap.

LMS Cl.4. 2-6-4T.

42083	Selby	8/6/52-6/7/52	Darlton.
42084	Darlton.	25/9/55-12/2/56	Whitby.
	Whitby	6/5/56-8/6/58	Whitby.
42085	Darlton.	25/9/55-12/2/56	Whitby.
	Whitby	6/5/56-8/6/58	Whitby.

LMS Cl.4. 2-6-0.

43052	New	10/8/50-1/7/51	Selby

LMS Cl.2. 2-6-0.

46409	Goole	21/1/62-7/10/62	Goole

LMS 0-6-0T

47403	York	13/9/59-26/9/61c	Scrap.

BR Standard Cl.5 4-6-0.

73167	Norman.	25/1/59-14/6/59	Norman.
73168	Leeds H.	25/1/59-14/6/59	Leeds H.
73169	Leeds H.	25/1/59-14/6/59	Leeds H.
73170	Leeds H.	25/1/59-14/6/59	Leeds H.

BR Standard Cl.3. 2-6-0.

77004	York	15/11/59-21/4/63	York.
77013	York	9/10/60-21/4/63	York.

BR Standard Cl.4. 2-6-4T.

80116	Whitby	12/2/56-6/5/56	Whitby.
80119	Whitby	12/2/56-6/5/56	Whitby.

BR Standard Cl.3. 2-6-2T.

82026	Darlton.	14/9/58-2/12/62	Low Moor.
82027	Malton	12/6/60-16/12/62	Malton.
82028	Darlton.	14/9/58-10/9/61	Malton.
82029	Malton	12/6/60-10/9/61	Malton.

By the end of September 1962 Scarborough engine shed had become something of a dump for redundant steam locomotives and twenty-two such engines were resident by the middle of that month:

A2	60515, 60516, 60518, 60522, 60526.
B16/3	61421, 61434, 61448, 61454, 61475.
J94	68046, 68061.
V2	60831, 60837, 60847, 60864, 60877.
WD	90030, 90045, 90078.
Cl.2	46409.
Cl.3	40117

As time went by these 'residents' were either withdrawn and towed away for scrap, or towed to another engine shed for further service.

Former London & North Eastern Railway locomotive numbers are presented as first/final number carried by engine during lifetime and not necessarily whilst allocated to Scarborough shed.

Abbreviations in table:

B.G. - Botanic Gardens;
Bor. Gdn. - Borough Gardens;
Cudwh. - Cudworth;
Dy. - Dairycoates;
Donc. - Doncaster;
Gateshd. - Gateshead;
Leeds H. - Leeds Holbeck;
Middsbr. - Middlesbrough;
Nev. - Neville;
N. Blyth - North Blyth;
Norman. - Normanton;
Richmd. - Richmond;
S. Blyth - South Blyth;
Sp. - Springhead;
Sunland. - Sunderland;
Tweed. - Tweedmouth;
Wakefd. - Wakefield;
W. Auck. - West Auckland;
W. Hart - West Hartlepool;
Yar. B. - Yarmouth Beach.

Key to table:

c - condemned.
scrap - engine went from Scarborough to scrap.
New - engine arrived from makers.
Those engines shown as 'Resident' were allocated to Scarborough shed at 1/1/23.

Not much change in this view from that of June 1953. It is now 2nd July 1955 and an Ivatt 4MT, No.43050, joins the throng on shed. One can only assume that the 2-6-0 is ready for a Whitby line goods working because this engine, along with others of its ilk - Nos.43051, 43054 and 43057 - were regular visitors from Middlesbrough. Our subject here was allocated to NER sheds throughout its life from new when it arrived at Darlington from its makers in July 1950. It ended its association with the North Eastern, and its life, in September 1967 at North Blyth when the whole of the region's steam locomotion was condemned. Scarborough had a single example of the class allocated from August 1950 until July 1951 when No.43052 arrive new from Doncaster works - it moved on to Selby.

Having arrived at Scarborough with a train via the coast line from Whitby, Middlesbrough based V3 No.67638 has just attended to its fuel situation at the coaling stage before continuing with the servicing procedure at the shed on 26th July 1952. It will next visit the turntable so that it can run home chimney first - the comfortable way. The south entrance to the old roundhouse is just beyond and the 2-6-2T will enter that building shortly in order to make use of the 44ft turntable therein, the total wheelbase of the V3, indeed its entire length easily fitting the turntable's dimensions. Once turned, the engine could slip out of the north entrance of the roundhouse and then reverse onto the yard without getting in the way of any other motive power also going through servicing. The pit wall of the depot's 60ft outside turntable, for the tender engines, can be seen on the right of the illustration.

Peppercorn K1 No.62008 from Darlington shed graces the shed yard on 2nd August 1952. How it arrived in Scarborough is unknown but it does not appear to be returning by way of the coast line and the Whitby route.

Another visitor to Scarborough was this Stanier Cl.5, No.45238, which had brought in the 8.31 a.m. from Bradford (Forster Square) on Saturday 23rd July 1955. The 4-6-0 was a recent addition to the Holbeck allocation having transferred from Burton earlier in the month.

Earlier on that July Saturday in 1955, this smartish looking A5 was spotted working back from the carriage sidings and making its way to shed for turning via one of the two-way independent lines. The 4-6-2T had worked in on the 8.42 a.m. from Stockton, where it had resided since the previous summer. Its last major overhaul had been undertaken at Gorton during September and October 1954 which does not account for its reasonable external condition which can only be put down to the cleaners at Stockton.

Shed pilot for the day - well until we've changed the empties over. York based B16/3 No.61434 propels four loaded coal wagons up the incline to the coaling stage during the engine's layover at Scarborough shed. It is a Saturday and the seasonal traffic has all but dried up now so using a 4-6-0 on work such as this would give the disposal crew some practice and keep them busy. As can be seen, the incline ran parallel with the fence separating the depot from Seamer Road and as coaling stage inclines go, this one was quite gentle having a long run (nearly a fifth of a mile) from the bottom, alongside the straight road engine shed, to the top which was adjacent to the entrance of the original roundhouse shed. Note that by now the stage did not posses a roof nor covering of any kind; a small garden shed-like wooden hut sufficed as mess-come-office for the coaling gang. The date is 3rd October 1953 and Scarborough shed did not posses any suitable tank engines at this time which could have performed this job more efficiently if perhaps less gracefully.

So, what's the problem? BR Standard Cl.3 No.77004, two D49s and another engine queue to get on shed on 23rd July 1955. Having to wait for each stage of the disposal routine to be carried out on each and every visiting engine must have sapped the patience of footplate crews alike but many was the time when the depot's own disposal gang would carry out the work allowing the 'day trippers' a chance to visit some of the attractions on offer at Scarborough. The trouble was getting the engine on shed in the first place! The 2-6-0 had of course arrived from Darlington and was a regular visitor to the seaside. Its crew would be eager to complete the shed servicing ready for their return working which would be listed on the timetable long before the excursions were due to depart.

Two earlier arrivals for shed room that Saturday were B16/3 No.61472 (which only turned ready to work the 'Flyer' as illustrated previously) and B1 No.61023 HIROLA, both of which had arrived light engine from York as part of a regular summer Saturday duty which extended to two and sometimes three such workings on some days. The B16 had completed a Heavy General overhaul just ten weeks previously but its external appearance belies that fact whilst on shed a cleaner clings to the side of A8 No.69878 trying to achieve the hopeless. The B1 was a recent addition to York's large fleet of 4-6-0s, having transferred from Darlington to help out with the summer traffic. Those were the days!

The next batch of light engines from York arrive alongside the shed on the morning of 23rd July 1955. Headed by D20 No.62381 we have an Ivatt 4MT and a B1 - basically Scarborough was sent anything that worked. Soon the first excursions will start arriving from far and wide so it was a matter of '...lets get this lot on shed and turned ready for whatever we throw at them...' In case anyone is wondering about the locomotives illustrated here, Selby shed was also involved in supplying motive power to Scarborough as part of the summer Saturday scheme.

Scarborough engine shed, Monday morning, 25th July 1955. A couple of A8s and a D49 grace the yard. The 4-4-0, No.62770 THE PUCKERIDGE is a local engine having transferred from Neville Hill to Scarborough in July 1948. It was to stay at the seaside until June 1959 when there was no longer a requirement for its presence and it was sent off to Selby in search of work. Unsuccessful there, it moved on to York in September but was condemned ten days later, not quite twenty-five years old. But before that catastrophic event, and the scene enacted here, No.62770 attended Gateshead works (an unusual venue for this class) for a Heavy General overhaul in January 1957. Of the two Pacifics, No.69886 was a local whilst No.69878 was a visitor from Middlesbrough. Note that both tanks are facing north in order to work services along the line to Whitby and beyond chimney first. The shed in picture is the eight-road straight shed and overleaf is a brief description of the motive power facilities available at Scarborough.

Later on during that Monday morning of 25th July 1955, the Selby based D20, No.62381, came onto the shed again for stabling, after turning and servicing ready for its journey back home later in the day. This particular 4-4-0 was not quite fifty years old at this time but it did manage to make the half-century whilst allocated to Botanic Gardens shed in March 1957. The Hull depot did not prove to be its last home either and in late September 1957 it travelled north to Alnmouth where its five surviving classmates had congregated too. That particular shed turned out to be the final place offering work to the six D20s because in November of that year the whole class was condemned and later cut up at Darlington.

How did all these trains get to Scarborough? Well here is one of the main arteries but illustrated is a train leaving the district on 18th June 1955. B1 No.61068, one of the Botanic Gardens allocation, departs from Seamer with the 8.15 a.m. Scarborough (Central) to Hull (Paragon) express. Look at the formation which is a tidy train for the Thompson 4-6-0 but easily within its capabilities. Although spending much of its early life in Hull, this particular engine transferred to Scarborough in June 1959 for a nine-month stint before moving on to Darlington at the end of March 1960.

Going onto the north side of town we come to another artery, this being the Whitby line and used mainly by scheduled services - both passenger and freight. Excursions from the north, especially the long and heavy formations originating in Scotland, tended to run via Gilmoor and the necessary reversal at Gilling rather than chance their luck on the coastal route with its rather undulating and unforgiving gradients. The route was, for much of its length single line to boot! However, the local services to and from Whitby, and those beyond to Middlesbrough, had adequate motive for their lightly loaded trains which at the heaviest in the summertime rarely exceeded five vehicles. This is V3 No.67638 approaching Gallows Close with the 7.30 a.m. all stations from Middlesbrough to Scarborough on 12th May 1956. The coast line north of here is single track and the line to the left terminated in Northstead carriage sidings.

BR Cl.3 No.77013 approaches Gallows Close with the 8.02 a.m. working from Darlington via the coastal route on 2nd July 1955. This was another Darlington based engine which, along with sister No.77014, was soon to become part of the small Whitby stud and would serve that shed until its closure. Once it had set down its passengers at Central (platform 1A no doubt), No.77013 would proceed to stable its four coach formation in the Down carriage sidings, situated just south of the engine shed. The two Standard Cl.3 2-6-0s featured in this album would one day become part of the Scarborough locomotive stud but with their arrival came the end of more than fifty years of steam excursions, 'foreign' locomotives, superb, ancient and varied coach formations, the knotted handkerchief and much more as Britain changed from one era to another. For better or worse? Who knows?